OTHER BOOKS IN THE SERIES:

Cat Jokes   **Golf Jokes**

Over 50s' Jokes   **Over 60s' Jokes**

Over 70s' Jokes   **Over 80s' Jokes**

OTHER BOOKS BY HELEN EXLEY:

Dogs 365   **The little book of Smiles**   **Be happy!**

Cats 365   **Senior Moments 365**   **For a friend**

Published in 2020 by Helen Exley ®LONDON in Great Britain.
Design, selection and arrangement © Helen Exley Creative Ltd 2020.
Illustrated by Roland Fiddy © Helen Exley Creative Ltd 2020.
All the words by Pam Brown copyright © Helen Exley Creative Ltd 2020.
The moral rights of the authors have been asserted.

12 11 10 9 8 7 6 5 4 3 2 1
ISBN: 978-1-78485-271-9

Helen Exley ® LONDON,
16 Chalk Hill, Watford, Herts, WD19 4BG, UK
www.helenexley.com

MIX
Paper from
responsible sources
FSC® C015559

Dog
quotes

WRITTEN BY PAM BROWN
ILLUSTRATIONS BY ROLAND FIDDY
EDITED BY HELEN EXLEY

Helen Exley

One looks
at a sleeping puppy
and forgives it
everything.

How peaceful
the sound
of a small dog snoring.

Nirvana must be
very like a replete
puppy's sleep.
A rapture beyond dreams.

Humankind is drawn
to dogs because
they are so
like ourselves –
bumbling, affectionate,
confused,
easily disappointed,
grateful for kindness...

Every dog deserves
a smile, a word of
admiration, a little
reassurance –
especially if he is
really ugly or very sad.

Give a dog
your love
and he will
give you his life.

How can I serve you?
asks Dog.

A dog meeting
its new owner says
"I love you.
Please, please, please
love me too."

People love dogs
because they
love them back.
Unconditionally.

...to lose all

loneliness

To hold a living creature,
to learn its loveliness,
to feel its heart beat in our hands,
To know trust is to
understand that we are kin,
is to rejoice in life.
Is to lose all loneliness.

A dog's greatest
desires in life
are to love
and be loved.

A dog loves you right or wrong.

The saddest thing about dogs
is their ability to forgive.

Most dogs
will declare undying,
everlasting adoration
at the sight
of a cream cake.

Your little dog
gulps down his food.
Before the hyenas
and the vultures arrive.

"I love you,
love you,
love you"
says Dog.
With dinner in mind.

A dog can never
get out of its head
how comfortable it was
to drift to sleep curled
on a human knee.
And goes on trying
to repeat the joy
– even when it is grown
and no longer fits.

Your dog
just doesn't notice
that you are old
or ill or
unsuccessful.
To him
you are perfect.

Don't worry.
Your dog thinks
you're wonderful
Your dog *knows*
you're wonderful.

You've lost your looks,
your money and your health.
But Dog declares you perfect.
Which brings a sort of comfort.

We must choose
the strongest pup,
the cleverest,
the most active.
So why do we choose,
the most helpless,
tiny, tiny dog,
all eyes
and rumpled fur?

No, Madam,
I am not a Pekinese.
Nor yet a Schitzu.
Nor yet a terrier
gone wrong.
I am utterly unique.
I am the Family Pup.

Most dogs don't thin
they know they are.

hey are human;

The little one, the wobbly one,
the one you have to carry round,
buttoned into your cardigan –
the one that's going to cost
a fortune in vet's bills.
The one who's car sick.
The one who panics every time
there's a knock – and would
flatten itself under the bed in silent
terror if there was a burglar.
The one you're going to keep.

THE
WOBBLY
ONE

A dog friend
just doesn't care
who you are –
fat or old or
none too steady
on your pins.
Just so long
as you love him.

The trouble
with a very
happy puppy
is that it leaks.

There are two sorts of puppies.
Those who declare they
have absolutely no idea
where the puddle came from.
And those who are plunged
into guilt and abject apology
by their awful deed.

Don't scowl, Missus.
I'm a very, very little puppy.
And it was a very,
very little pee.

Your dog
still believes
in you when
everyone else
has given up.

Here is a little life
within the house.
A creature to love and care for.
Dependent on our will.
A dog, giving us his life in trust.
Do not betray him.
He has so much to give.
So much to teach.

"Beg!" I say.
"Sit!" I say.
"Down!" I say.
And he smiles
– and wanders off.

Bad dog.
Go to your basket.
And so he does,
turns thrice around.
Springs out smiling,
penance done.

There is nothing so guilty as a guilty dog.

When a dog has done
something diabolical,
he is racked with guilt –
and so gives
the game away.

How small,
how helpless,
how utterly
gormless
a puppy is.

A puppy yearns
with every single part
of its being to serve
and love you.
Love it in return.
Never betray its trust,
never despise its loyalty
– or misuse it.

TRUST

A dog trusts even those
who do not deserve his love.
If someone repays his trust
they have a friend for life.

When you feel
pretty worthless –
your dog will reassure you.

When the rest of the family
are scowling
– your dog is on your side.

A dog loves to share hi

fe, and his joys with you.

A dog
cannot read print,
but he can read
your eyes, your mouth,
your fingertips,
very well indeed.

Dog needs no words.
"Scratch me here –
and here.
Now rub my belly,
pull my ears.
Pat me and tell me
I am wonderful."

I am old and tired, blind and nearly deaf.
But, once, long, long ago, I was a pup
and won the woman's heart.
And so we have shared the years together
living in each other's love.
And will do till the end.
For while I have her love
this life I live is good –
and when I grow too weary
she will come with me to the edge
of the welcoming dark
– most wise, most kind, most caring
– most sorrowful, that we at last must part.
For I am her pup, her dog,
her companion and her friend.

forever

friends

To take a young dog on

One's quiet, obedient, placid dog
let off the leash on a rabbit-haunted
common is transformed.
Races and turns, twists,
flourishes his tail,
dives through broom and fern, snuffles
into burrows. Pursues the invisible.
Is free as the wind.
Is utterly alive.
Is the everlasting Dog.

ill walk is to share delight.

A dog begs for a tit bit.
Begs to be carried.
Begs at the bus stop
Begs at the butchers.
Who needs language?

That lady very near us
on the beach
has sweeties.
Just hang on a minute
while I put on
my Pitiful Pose.

In desolation
a dog can be
a lifeline
to a wider,
kindlier world.

A dog
will continue
to trust
when it has
been
betrayed.

Some dogs, having endured
appalling suffering,
are so broken kindness
can never cure them.
And some come out of horror
still capable of trust and love
and find at last
the world a happy place.

A dog can fill a yawning chasm
in your life.

Here's lov

Disguised as a mop.

Adog is utterly convinced
that you are the wisest,
kindest and most skilful person
in the world.

Your dog think.

You may be Just You
to the rest of the family.
To your dog you're
the heart of the Universe.

you're perfect.

The dog has stolen
the roast off your table.
He has hidden himself away.
He's just waiting for you
to forgive him,
to love him again.

A repentant, frightened dog
is one of the saddest sights
you will ever, ever see.

I am not coming out
from under the bed –
not ever – until you turn
the thunder off.

Little dogs left outside shops
are frantic or despairing or resigned.
Or simply quietly miserable.
They watch the door.
And turn ecstatic at the sight of Her
– leaping and spinning, nuzzling, kissing,
wagging everything it's possible to wag.
She is half embarrassed by such rapture
– but glad to know that a little pat
will put its world to rights.

A dog tied up
outside a shop
is a dog
convinced that
he has been
abandoned
forever.

The dog has been
our companion
for so long
to ill treat him
is betrayal.

New owners of small dogs are
determined to be kind, but firm,
to establish the proper pecking order,
to instil obedience.
To make quite sure that the puppy
knows its place.
So there they are. Food bowl.
Basket. Blanket. Pup. In the kitchen.
Anxious owners snug in bed,
door shut – and,

for the puppy's sake,
hardening their hearts.
It takes the pup an hour or two –
but, with luck, only half an hour –
of sobbing, wailing, howling, moaning,
whimpering, of scrabbling, thumping
and shoving things around.
Before it is curled up on the bed.
Just for tonight.
Or the next fifteen years.

A lost dog
is one of the most
pitiable of creatures.
And so afraid,
he is beyond reason.

A lonely dog i

"Won't be long"
means nothing to a dog.
All he knows
is that you are
GONE.

desolate dog.

A dog knows that if he sits in front of you long enough and pleads with every look and wag – you'll eventually give in and take him for a walk.

"I know it's snowing hard.
I know there's something
special on the television.
But my clock says, Walkies."

ies!

A dog who has just been bathed is a dog looking for a filthy patch in which to roll.

Dogs love to share mud, water, nameless, awful objects.

A dog who has
just rolled in a cowpat
is especially
affectionate.

A dull day, a sad day,
a frustrating day –
but everything seems
bright when a small furry
object hurls into your arms
and tells you how very glad
he is to see you home.

The nearest thing

to being hit

by a cannon ball

is being greeted

by a Staffy.

sin

Peter's practicing the piano.
I'll sing along.

There's nothing
some dogs like better
than to join in
and sing.

Innoc

ence!

One can teach
even a tiny dog discipline.
"Go in your basket"
says Master in his sternest voice.
And the puppy obeys.
Enters the basket, tail down,
turns round a time or two
– and then leaps out
beaming from ear to ear
and prances over for a pat
– a virtuous and obedient dog.

"Go to your bed,
you bad, bad dog!"
And so he would,
crawling across the carpet
on his belly, ears down,
abject.
Once in his basket,
however,
he would take one brisk
turn-round and jauntily
re-join us.
All forgiven
and forgotten.

Wash your dog – an

Water features?
Nothing compared
to a very wet dog
shaking himself dry.

tand well back.

A dog can
nearly drown you
as he shakes
himself dry.

For most a dog is
a good companion.
For some he is
their guide,
their protector
– their friend,
their life.

One of the
greatest mysteries
in human evolution
is how and why dogs
felt the necessity
to build
close relationships
with other species –
not as servants,
but companions.
Friends.

I don't know how to use a litter tray
or to bury my garden messes.
I can only go out of the yard on a leash
And I bark at everything.
I'm not very good at washing myself.
And I roll in doubtful substances.
I cock my leg up other peoples' cars.
And I smell a bit iffy in warm weather
But I love you, love you, love you,
and I will go on loving you
till the day I die.
…till the day I die.

A dog deprived
of a pack,
however small,
is a lost dog.
Be his pack.

A puppy
is so apologetic
for his sins
you are obliged
to forgive him.

forgive

ness

A dog listens
to your sorrows.
He may not completely
understand but he knows
you need him
close and warm and loving.

A dog will say,
whatever your troubles,
"Never mind.
You've always got me."

You've fallen flat.
Dog is worried.
Can I give you a hand?
Should I fetch the vet?
Would licking help?
My teddy bear?
A bone?

Nothing is so joyful
as a wagging tail.

In lacking a tail
we humans are restricted
in the expression of joy.

A happy

A happy dog
wags not only
its tail
– but every bone
and sinew.

dog

The saddest thing
about dogs
is that they love
where love
is not deserved.

A dog can bid you a cheerful goodbye
– but look through the letter box
ten minutes later
and you'll find he's probably sitting,
head well back,
eyes rolled to heaven,
howling for your return.

The dog pens at rescue centres
rend the heart.
They are so full of hope
and desperation.

What a very small,
what a very ordinary dog.
No pedigree
and very little looks –
But a creature
full of life and love.

You can never be as wonderful
as your dog thinks you are
– but he at least is convinced.

A dog greets you:
Hello! You're back!
I love you,
love you,
love you.
Let me kiss your ear.
Let me nuzzle your hands.
Let me wag
and roll and scamper.

Dogs come in
hundreds of varieties.
They have one thing
in common.
The capacity
to love us.

A dog is love

A dog asks for very little
A warm bed,
fresh water,
his supper
– and a kiss
on the nose.

or a lifetime.

You can't very well blame him.
In sorting out what it is
and what isn't edible any pup
can make mistakes.
And he really doesn't know
the cost of cushions.

When he's got to bury a bone,
he's got to bury a bone.
"Sorry Dad.
I didn't notice the petunias."

Your dog
may well
bring you
the newspaper.
What's left of it.

A dog shouts
"Rain! Snow! Hurricane!
Let's go for walk!"

"Walk."
"Now."
"See, that's my lead.
This is the door.
Pull yourself together, Dad.
Can't you see
that this is very,
very urgent?"

A dog is jubilant
at the sight
of his lead.

A life,
a warmth,
an intelligence.
A kind companion.
A dog.

Your dog assures
that you'll never lack
a friend.

One of the most
extraordinary things in life
is that we can
become close friends
with creatures of
another species.
Their friendship
increases our perception
and teaches us
how to respect them.

A dog does not help merely by being soft and warm and alive, but by telling the human being that it does not matter if she or he is old or ugly, helpless or confused. It does not matter that they have failed, if they are poor, or that the world seems to have no further use for them. An animal sees the self that has never changed since it was new born, the young soul that occupies the old or injured body.

Dog says
"With me around
you can never
be lonely."

Give a pup
a home and
a little love
and he will give
you his heart
forever.

Even a puppy
will endure
the unendurable
out of love.

A pup is like
a baby. It goes
on trusting
long after it has
been betrayed.

A dog
is all heart.
And
stomach.

A dog desires
affection more than
its dinner.
Well – almost.

Dogs love plum cake
and affection equally.
And the average dog
does not so
much eat his food
as vacuum it.

To buy a pup
is to invest in love.

A pup brought up
in a loving family
believes that everyone
is lovable and that
they all adore very small,
bouncy, licky dogs.

A dog can only live
if it can love.

Puppies are chewin

You have to make the decision.
Carpets and chair legs,
china and glass and cushions,
saplings and seedlings and garden hoses.
Slippers and hand-stitched shoes.
Or the puppy.

Dear Master –
here's your slipper back.
I've finished with it now.

nachines.

It is wonderful how much
one small puppy
can chew and destroy
in an afternoon alone.

An abandoned dog,
however small,
is totally contented
just being loved,
being wanted,
being your companion.

Whoever else thinks
you are of little worth –
to your dog
you are the heart
of his universe.

A puppy lives
every second
of its life with
total commitment.

Dog delights
in giving you delight.

A mud-caked dog
is the most affectionate dog
in the world.
Especially if you
are dressed to the nines.

Any wet dog feels boun

Stand clear of the dog
emerging from the river.
He has brought most of it
with him.

A dog is
a hundred times
more demonstrative
when he's soaking wet
and muddy
than when he's dry.

share his mud.

If your dog
decides it is time
for his walk –
there's not a great deal
you can do about it.

If friends fail us and
the phone is silent,
your dog will touch your knee,
and smile, and say,
"All the more time for us to be together.
Come for a walk.
This is a splendid day."

Dogs requiring a walk
will take you
to the coat cupboard
and make
the matter clear.

"Fetch!"

"Who? Me?"

The doors swing open – and her face
lights up in incredulous joy.
"You're a silly dog, then.
Aren't you a silly dog?
I told you I wouldn't be long."
This to a squirm of back,
a flash of paws, a lashing of tail,
a bucketing rump, a leap
and a wriggle and a lolling tongue.
For both of us
the world has come right again.

You come home.

The dog throws itself at you.

"Where have you been?

You've been so long.

I missed you, missed you, missed you.

I love you, love you, love you.

What's in the bag? Something for me?

Oh, let me lick your ear.

You're HOME!"

Dogs have stolen ou
and our hearts.

omes, our food

A dog's paws
are designed to carry
enough wet mud
to decorate
the entire house.

A dog's world is an ecstasy of smells.
And, lovingly, he likes
to share them.
Manure and creosote
being his special gifts.

A dog that has been frolicking
in mud looks for somewhere
to dispose of it.
Scrubbed floors, clean carpets, bed.
Missus.

A dirty dog
is a happy dog.

Squibs, like most dogs,
hated to be bathed.
Spotless, dry
and smelling good,
he would, of course,
immediately go out to find
somewhere most rancid
in which to roll.

Dogs have
uncomplicated souls.
Their needs are few.
Food.
A place to sleep.
You.

A pup does not know words.
It just hears love.

Dogs fall in love
without discrimination.

Dogs love you –
warts and all.

Choose the boldest,
the bravest,
the brightest, they say.
But who is the one
at the back, all fur and eyes
and desperation?
Willing you to notice her.
Willing you
to take her home.

We may not be able to speak Dog – but dog understands us.

Your dog will worry
about your welfare
and do what he can to help.

You've been away.
Dog forgives in an instant.
Welcome Home.
I love you, love you, love you.

A dog can talk
you into most things
– silently.

A puppy is convinced
that life is good
– and always will be.
Never disillusion him!

A happy dog

A dog running
for joy of living
is happiness
personified.

radiates joy.

A dog can be more
than a companion
in pain and loss
and loneliness.
It can be a friend
and comforter.

A dog can add years
to an old person's life
– someone to care for,
someone to come home to,
someone to talk to
A dear friend.

A dog smiles
with its whole face,
ears,
eyes,
nose,
whiskers,
mouth,
tongue.

A dog is a smile
and a wagging tail.
What is in between
doesn't matter much.

A smiling dog
makes everyone
smile back.

A funny fellow

The daft dog
is often the most dearly loved.

A dear dog.
A loving dog.
A companionable dog.
And thick
as two short planks.
But that is all
I ever wanted.

There is invariably one dimwit
in the litter – but what he lacks
in wisdom he usually makes up for
in bumbling charm.

There is absolutely nothing
like a kindly Mutt.